LOTTERY OF INTIMACIES

JONATHAN KATZ

POETRY

C&R Press
Conscious & Responsible

Cover art by Tarmo Watia
Interior design by Jojo Rita

ISBN 978-1-949540-24-6
LCCN 2021939664

C&R Press
Conscious & Responsible
crpress.org

For special discounted bulk purchases, please contact:
C&R Press sales@crpress.org
Contact info@crpress.org to book events, readings and author signings.

LOTTERY OF INTIMACIES

For Bob Lynch and Dianne Brace
with admiration and affection

I grew to value whatever gifts I drew
in the lottery of intimacies,
knowing that a view of me
in a stranger's eyes without my shirt,
flexing and full of triumph,
in every ironic context
of age and death and treason,
would be the price for playing the game
and loving it beyond reason.

---from "Treason," *Love Undefined*

CONTENTS

The Occasional Poem

Bubbles

News from Leicestershire

It is difficult
to get the news from poems
          yet men die miserably every day
                    for lack
of what is found there.

---W. C. Williams, "Asphodel, that Greeny Flower"

NEWS FROM LEICESTERSHIRE

Good week for: Eternal devotion, after archaeologists in
Leicestershire, England, uncovered a pair of skeletons in a
church graveyard that were still holding hands after nearly 700
years in the ground.

              ---*The Week*, October 3, 2014

They had heard about the nuisance as far south
as Wigston and as far north as Loughborough,
not just the pushing and fighting and yelling,
because all the villages had couples who
just couldn't take a break and let their momentary
differences simmer down, just stamp the fire
underneath the kettle out and fetch something
or count how far the sun moved in the sky
during a trip to the wood and back, how long
that took, but this was the stuff of stories,
how once she ran him naked round the pig pen
with a pitchfork in broad daylight and the animals
escaped and all the neighbors had to run them down---
the boars, sows, piglets and the woman, and
another when he smacked her so hard you could see
the mark upon her forehead for a week.
They said it must have been like that for Cain
and sure she was a sinner also, then another
when she broke the pitcher on his shoulder
and another when he threw the soup then threw
the bowl at her as well, so then she took the ladle
to him, and he ran into a neighbor's stable,
spooked the horses, twice she moved in with her
sister and her brother-in-law for a few days,
but always she went back, that reason never
understood, any more than whom this fall
St. Anthony's fire would drive mad,
and stories traveled, growing always
with some new details of the teller's
mulled imagination. It was because the whole

thing was so frequent, and so public, and
such trouble for the village as a group,
when finally he got the bloody flux and died
"She's free for good" was what the people said,
but then she didn't last a month, a cough
and fever took her, seemed that all her fight
was gone. The dirt above the husband
was still soft. The neighbors got the sister
and her man drunk, some agreed to watch
them sleep, the others stole out to the cemetery,
dug the grave up, and they placed the bodies
hand in hand, giggling as they labored.
"Just the same as ever,"
said a smart-mouthed smithy.
"Forever lovers!" said another; with a laugh
they all repeated it: "Forever lovers!"
and covered them in their new bed
and patted down the dirt much harder
this time with their shovels. It felt good
the next day at the tables and around the fires.
They did not put it into words,
but there is something satisfying
in completion of a task that ends a story
in a way that nothing will change ever,
in that feeling of the power of a story teller.
When the minstrel from the west arrived
that year he brought the stunning news:
a dray horse had been seen to fly in Coventry.

HEARD ON THE RELIGION AND MATHEMATICS RADIO HOUR

Your findings on the math problem may be difficult
to estimate or verify since fingers come in five's and ten's.
The nine-branched menorah blooms candles for eight nights.
Each evening, you see, the extra one lights up the others.
Since what prayers measure is not weight or number,
there is some division on whether it's your fault
the image of that stern yet sexy choir teacher lingers.
The Lord loves you in spite of a sundry wrong answer
you might give to a math problem, but predestination
is a different proposition we will take up elsewhere.

This is all I recall, which is probably a good thing,
because I read last week that literary magazines nowadays
prefer to publish poems that leave interpretation
for the reader to do rather than wrap things up
neatly with some kind of logical or rhetorical ribbon.
Plus, I might have dreamt instead of heard that Radio Hour.

MAIN COURSE

Op het karkas gebakken tamme duivenborst
met in bokbierbeslag gefrituurde batonnets
van bleekselderij en een gestoofd appeltje

Supreme of tamed pigeon sautéed en chemise
in batter of bock beer with bâtonettes
of blanched celery and a stewed apple

Once it was that bird that annoyed you
with its lusty gurglings,
defeating your pedestrian imagination
with the mechanics of how it could
actually accomplish the sex it wanted,
and crapping all over your car,
whether you parked it under a tree
or within spitting distance of a building ledge.

How did they tame it?
Death is only where the process begins.
When and where they killed it is not meaningful.
They dressed it in a little chemise
and pushed it around in a very hot pan;
they boiled the color out of erect celery
and issued a pale arsenal of miniature batons;
they dummied it up like a high school drum major
overdosed, sharing its wake with a stewed apple.

You know I take my role as poet very seriously
and, right about now, you can see
what a mixed blessing that is for all of us—
but I digress. The bird is the thing.
Palatable as it becomes, the questions
cling like bock beer batter:
What can a pigeon do anyway
without being offensive to someone?

And, is it really fair to treat an animal
the same way we treat people?

On the other hand, we do need recipes
and recipes imply certain premises
and premises lift their skirts
to ask how their legs look, don't they?

So, Lesson one:
> you can't keep crapping on people with impunity.

Lesson two:
> not everyone wants to hear about your sex life.

Lesson three:
> people get excited taming the wildness of others.

Lesson four:
> no matter what shape you are in,
> show a little style and someone will think you delicious.

There are other lessons here, I'm sure—
when is the work of a poem really done?
For instance: how easy it is to die,
to be summed up in a few lines,
to be translated into language you would not even recognize
and to have your death accepted.

But, oh, those darling chemises and vainglorious celery bâtonettes!
They can make you cry.

WATCHING THE NEIGHBORS' DOG

take a dump
is one of the most pleasurable experiences
this world has to offer, especially
when you're taking a dump yourself
and looking out your second floor window
below the screen and can't be seen
and the animal strains, finishes,
steps proudly forward, kicks back
a few times, and just frolics, transforming
the lawn, which my neighbor, not I,
and, most to the point, not the dog,
will have to clean up, into an Eden
of pure unselfconscious joy.

I realize this tells you a little about me
but the real audience for this poem
are the alien scholars and scientists
who arrive eons hence and commence
to reconstruct and try to figure out our world.
I'm sure they'll have their pantheon
of pleasures, some of which relate to ours:
some sense of preference for tasting
one nutrient over others, and some intimate
sensory incentive to promulgate the species.
Responsibilities also I expect they will have---
tribal, civic and familial, and a galaxy of commerce,
but just how similar to ours it's difficult to say.

That's why I think we have to put the real deal
on the table. If we don't animate the kind
of moment that makes life on earth
worthwhile beyond the uptick of a stock
or the allure inviting procreation,
they might never know we were,
in fact, their kin, or whether something basic,

something like a universal peccadillo
necessary to the understanding of us,
had vanished with our bodies
and was lost forever.

OVERTURNING THE HORSESHOE CRAB

When my father dashed away from us
across the street to separate a man
from the wife he was berating and
brow-beating and possibly about to hit,
I watched my mother. She was furious.
He had abandoned us, put at risk our
breadwinner, for what? Not our family;
not even friends. Was a child in the picture
over there? Maybe so, but some woman
was the issue at hand and, if something
went wrong, who would take care of us?
Was this woman in any way special?
The man was my father's size, but only
determination was etched on my father's
face, jaw forward, eyes wide, arms pumping.
I knew he had been in the army. I didn't
know what he was still fighting. My
mother yelled "Joey, Get back here!
Mind your own business!"
It struck me she was more than angry.
She thought him a fool.

At Gerritsen Beach, near our house,
the child I became would pick up
the dead horseshoe crab
and turn the leathery armor over
to inspect the insides, the legs,
and to look for the brain, as if the
ancient machinery were a puzzle
assembled over millions of years
as a test for the new guy,
a tutorial of ingenuity.
I wondered how hard
I would have to shake it
to understand what it means to be alive,
to feel its primitive passions,
to sense a thought on the way.

Fire, I have been instructed, has several
characteristics of life. Irritability, one is
called, the interaction and response to
external stimuli. It ingests nutrients
and grows. Who knows what it feels?
And anyway, feeling isn't necessary to live,
may in some ways be counter-productive.
To what uses, I wonder, do trees put feelings?
I've become one attentive to homeostasis,
the stable equilibrium of interdependent elements,
the criterion that eliminates fire from the family of life.

O kindred creatures sheltered by a shell,
O rivers of flame that flatten forests and view
all the world as fuel, O waters that flood and recede,
calve bergs, and, like a great digestive pool, brunch on reefs,
winds that warm and whirl, filter sun and irrigate the plain,
lands that feed and bury, shift, shake, separate and thrust,
please forgive how clumsily I'm turning over everything
to learn what new criteria connect us,
mind, matter and emotion, to breed and to breathe.

WORDS FROM WINNERS

Contestant #3, you wrote
I like for people to read my writing and think, hey,
that's me, or, I used to know someone like that.

Dear #3,
Hey, yes, I used to know someone like that;
like that, meaning someone like that person,
like that, meaning that's how I came to know them,
thinking, Hey, that's me, until I knew it wasn't.

Contestant #12, you wrote
Movies are a huge inspiration; my stories tend to be
somewhat cinematic, complete with soundtracks
and the requisite panning out.

Dear #12,
In the pond, among the muscular, inbred koi, the clouds float
or perhaps there are many, many gallons of cloudy water
holding up the lotus pads. Across the pond,
beyond the low arc of the wooden bridge,
is that a brush fire? In the shaft-lit shallows of memory,
what is the word for myriad images suspended like flecks of gold?
Requisite indeed. If you didn't pull the camera back,
we could only see smoke and motion,
only hear your swirling prayer.

Contestant #31, you wrote
The lucky thing about writing is that the sitting down to "create"
is really a very small part of it all. Living is the real—
and considerably more difficult—meat of the thing.

Dear #31,
The artist says, I do it and you think about it,
and the scholar replies, so you can do it better,
and the artist replies, this is boring.

And the scholar says, no it isn't; think about it,
and the artist says, get a life.
Regardless, you sit down to write and now
I'm living in a small universe of your things:
lucky and difficult and meat.

Contestant #54, you wrote
Much to my parents' dismay,
I can only guarantee them more writing
in which intimate details about themselves
are revealed to strangers.

Dear #54,
Gandhi's wife awoke to find
he'd given away her jewels
as demanded by his calling;
may you, too,
experience the blessings of virtue.

Contestant #87, you wrote
Writing in a second language meant that it was always a struggle
to say what I meant, and the struggle was good.

Dear #87,
If it were easy to say what we mean,
who would struggle to write a poem?
I try to say let me help you however inept I may be
I believe that my loving intention will find a way
and it comes out whadda you mean I no toll you
da horse wuzza bline; you no heara me say
it no looka so good? If feelings
are prisoners held at the border,
then words are like foreign officials
you don't know whether to flatter or bribe,
winking and nodding slanderous signals
half hidden behind their fabulous silken fans.

Having betrayed my own parents
by projecting their actions and focusing judgments
through my eyes, I struggle when I vision them
peering down from eternity at my treason
and wonder what, Contestant #87,
you would say to Contestant #54's dismayed parents,
and to my own,
their intimate hopes and frustrations displayed
like graffiti tagging a random wall along a throughway,
struggling to find the language,
wanting to be proud that they have born a winner.

THE HOUNDS OF LIDO BEACH

When life is sweet and its lights shine brightest
it casts the scariest shadows on the walkways and walls.
The loved one waving from the gate
increases tenfold my dread of boarding the plane.
Also, I am worried that the good life on the West Coast,
the West Coast of Florida, that is, would be so easy
and friendly and white sandy and that green-blue
color of the languid Gulf water that it would be
difficult to sustain my hard, creative edge.
The start of my concern was when I learned
it took no more than a couple of glasses of Chardonnay
from the other West Coast before the canapes
at the botanic garden reception began to look
like trilobites and someone asked me if I wanted
a bite on a cracker and I laughed and laughed
because, you know, they meant the creamy brie
and not a taste of ancient arthropod, but that
was the thing crawling around in my head
and still tickling me at the next reception
that evening, which was at an art gallery
where the former musicians all knew the punchlines
to my trombone-player-as-loser jokes. Like they knew
that the difference between a dead possum
on the highway and a dead trombone player
was that the possum might have been on the way
to a gig, and they knew that what you call
a beautiful girl on the arm of a trombone player
is a tattoo. I recognize this giddy queasiness;
it's like the fear of loving someone too much.

Along the alluvial margin, the ibis dip
their down-bent beaks, the gulls, terns and plovers
seek morsels in the spume, the pelicans patrol
what skims and flashes underneath the waves
and so it seems the claps of the incessant crashes

are not overlapping slaps of tides receding
and tides coming in, but are the rumble of the air escaping
from the billion-bubbled foam, popping of a myriad
liquid corks, explosive invitation to the feeding birds
that little bugs and things without a spine are up for grabs.

I wish I could believe in, could accept
a peaceable interpretation of the world I see,
settle up and settle in comfortably
among tropical pleasures, engage the cruelty in nature,
unfairness, inequities, the pain of others
at my leisure, selectively, and not feel guilty,
not feel like some dilettante of misery.

Those tracks gouged into the sun-blanched silica sand,
I know they could be skewed and slanted forward
by the cadre of ambitious waiters carrying trays of mojitos,
but I am imagining anyway they mark the trail
of pounding paw prints, a muscular warning
to crepuscular walkers like me, who are stalked by
the maddening, mocking, strand-scavenging beasts
known only as The Hounds of Lido Beach.

DREAM TEAM

The dining hall was full and everyone
pretty well liquored up from the cocktail reception
when the guests of honor filed in to take their places
at the head table. No one expected each one
to say a few words in passing by the miked podium
but after the blind bard fumbled around a bit
and led off with a kind of invocation
no one else would be outdone. "Say, what has
six feet and lots of Homer hits?" was his opener
and people yelled out "dactylic hexameter" and
"the Iliad" and "the Odyssey" but when he said
"1927 Yankee Murderers Row---
Ruth, Gehrig, and Bob Meusel;
those dudes had homers out the wazoo!"
the crowd just fell apart with big guffaws
and slapping the table, and even though no one
remembered Bob Meusel, who had batted in
over a thousand runs and hit .309 lifetime,
it kind of set the tone.

Gerard Manley Hopkins reluctantly had to be
practically pushed up and mumbled he'd always failed
these kinds of tests, thought them worse than dying of typhoid,
which he also did not recommend, and specifically to avoid
this kind of occasion had burned a bunch of poems
that he intended as a wrung rent hand-mended garment
to be apprehended, unbent and returned more whole
to his cell, his Creator and his profligate soul.

Andre Breton seemed a bit distracted, apologized for being late,
had been walking under clouds, he said, that set him dreaming,
tilted that evening's world on its axis, corrupted the logic
of a ticking clock and scheduled destination with the freedom
of children and madmen. Amoral and loosened of any aesthetic,
a shirt lay on a floor, a large white flower bloomed over a field,
a ravaged box of chocolates sat upon a chair and the moon bled.

Breton looked DeNiro full in the face.
"I know *you* will understand," he said.
"The sky was *talking* to me.
It was talking to *me*!"

Borges said, "*I* quite understand, having viewed
this evening's path in two mirrors posing
an infinite fractal fiction of forking possibilities
to which any number of invented footnotes
might offer diversion until their own reality
engulfs human events down through history
from Ararat to Buenos Aires, time grows pure
in the plenitude of night, and we see what God
sees, the other side of the tapestry."

Blake and his entourage were clearly unaccustomed
to formal dining and his expressions of gratitude
were both profuse and an embarrassment, as if
the party could have claimed representation
of personalities so far outside of fashion they are in.
Blake's posse posed and vogued, those fantastic Zoas,
fiery Luvah, energetic nexus of love and war,
airy Urizen, author of measures and limits to vision,
watery Tharmos, empowered to connect or mystify
and earthy Urthona, who builds and crushes.
They loomed and lowered like a mash-up of Comic-Con,
Mixed Martial Arts, World Wrestling Entertainment
and the American Council of Learned Societies.
"*Opposition* is *true* friendship," Blake, summing up,
insisted, and though I did hear the words "wack job,"
"inconsistent internally" and "Looney Tunes,"
I also heard "This is the coolest guy in the room."

When the chef kindly stopped for her
Emily Dickinson told him she hoped for some thing
on the menu that used to have feathers.
She was not in a mood to say anything good,
but would not mind a table where half-rhymes were available
and passing the rumors du jour de rigueur.

Alice Roosevelt stood, said, "Sit here by me, sister.
Let's buzz us some flies" ---the poet felt she could trust her.

William Carlos Williams said he'd rather have eaten at home
for not much delight impends from the red veal and marrow
braised with kale beside the trite chicken;
Frost suggested one should get acquainted with each bite,
and Eliot waxed eloquent: "No grazing, sit
as if upon a burnished throne, though others hurry by,
let's chew the softened tubers slowly
you and I, try mustard spread upon the rye.
Be not impatient, eating fries that fell upon a table;
Be imagining the pleasures yet to water your dull roots
with memory and desire stirring in the pantry, pantry, pantry."

Sylvia Plath, Virginia Woolf and Anne Sexton
stood arm in arm while everybody held their breath
and felt the afternoon shadows begin to lengthen
as the women first whispered among themselves,
then smiled at friends and admirers in the audience,
remembering how envied they had been.
Dylan Thomas said to A.E. Housman,
"It never occurred to me not to grow old."
"Well," said Housman, "When the food at the fairground
tastes bad, you get angry. Some just get sad."
Said Edna St. Vincent Millay, "Enough drink
in my tank and I sing in my chains.
That's a price I am willing to pay."

It was my turn. I stood up.
My heart was a thunderstorm.

My lungs filled with breath
and I dove in the deep moment's whirlpool.
"Ladies and Gentlemen," I threw my arms open
to embrace one and all, even servers and cleanup,
"I awoke with the tongue of a thick ox
but, with a sound like the frightening mouths

of fragile salts, it rose in a regiment with those hands
that wild tobacco would adore and erected
a barricade the color of fury
like the invisible engine of heaven itself."
I knew I had the whole team's attention.
"It is you who inspire me, pistons the words
that impale melting seasons with a swallowing green
and downy white drifts, no one has heavier shoes
now than I do, I claim my own language Excalibur
out of whatever was gummy before, asteroids are
like so many twirling plates on sticks to me now.
Wake up my banker; the drinks are on me!"

I know I said something like that because
yesterday I got two irate calls, one from a
hotel accounts agent, one from a
financial customer service rep,
and I heard myself say, to each,
"I don't think the party with whom
you intend to communicate
speaks the same language, but I shall
attempt to convey the message
when opportunity nods like a whispering
would-be conspirator cloaked in a black hooded robe
beneath a bone-bright beacon moon about to wane.
Good day to you."

Well, thanks for the generous loan of your ears.
I would savor adorning them each with a gemstone
but I must be elsewhere---and now.
Please kindly convey
the nature of my regrets
to anyone with the sorry task
of asking after the likes of me.

THE OBJECT OF MY AFFECTION

I have a rush of uncontrollable affection
for the flight attendant gliding forward,
gliding back, leaning over now and then
to take away whatever I give,
because, unlike so many, many others,
this attentive one says thank you,
thank you for your trash.

My Attractive Nuisance

'What weather of heaven is this?'

'The storm, the storm of a kiss.'

---"Her Words," Theodore Roethke

MY ATTRACTIVE NUISANCE

I thought of the pool as mine because
technically it was my property but
the reality was that even though it wore
the guise of its rental agreement and
many gravitated to it, the liquid asset
had a life of its own, a demanding
biological and chemical rhythm,
its own relationships with wind
and leaves and everything that possibly
could dive, or slip or slice or stumble in.
I built a high, tight private fence
around it, latched the gate to keep
the less mature ones out, removed
the evidence its body had been frequently
mistreated, disrespected, viewed as a latrine
by spoiled, pleasure-seeking dilettantes,
who never will deserve to float into you.
I do. I have saved myself all year, let no
desire supersede the privilege of this moment.
Lesser athletes see themselves in motion or
suspended. I have earned an intimacy, sovereign
fealty, and am prepared to be absorbed
into the patient limpid embrace of the beloved.

THE AUTHOR'S DREAM

There was a boy ran all alone
right to the center of a forest
All the trees became his hair
His feet grew deep into the earth
and where had been his heart
a sparrow sits piping in the dark

All the cause of this was just a girl
who when she saw him walking in the wood
lay down each time along a stream that carried twigs
and always this had seemed to him a dream to which
the end must come, like ripples widening
in a tangent pool the current passes by
however pounding in his ears his heart
and white the foaming waters at the source

How like a dream that even as she spoke
he heard no sound above his heart
and so he thought that waking
he could put beyond recall
the treetops whirling in the silent wind

Not the green bud on the icy branch
nor all the leaves next spring
in the moist wind waving
distract the author writing out his fate

And so a boy runs all alone
right to the center of a forest
All the trees become his hair
His feet grow deep into the earth
and where had been his heart
a sparrow sits piping in the dark

THE LAWN

The strong gusts blew the long,
white drapes like ghosts over our heads.
Though she had no face yet, my future
wife was running up the lawn's long grass
waving her arms and my father
set his jaw and scowled as he
dialed my number. You and I
were naked, rolling on the rough
living room carpeting, slamming into
the wall, spilling ashtrays onto
our flung clothes, rolling over butts
and buckles, biting, pulling,
curtain rods and drapes were falling,
sunlight poured into the room, the
phone was ringing, hands were flailing at and pounding
on the door, we were rolling over books
and letters, cackling, chanting
La La La to wordless tunes but loud
I think because you were to leave
in the late afternoon and our eyes had only lately met;
also, it had been for each of us so long.... .
When all the knocking had stopped,
after our whispering and your quiet humming,
and you had gone for good,
I stepped across the dangling charger cord
to the window, my future wife's footprints
in bent and broken dandelions indelible on the lawn,
and I thought how the wind would carry
a lasting dampness, but when I would next get around
to cutting the lawn, the sharp, green smell would rise magnificent.

BABYLON

"How shall we sing the Lord's song in a foreign land?"

--- Psalm 137

We meet to eat once or twice and each time
go out after, but without significance.
It seems that you call it Babylon
for all the whoring that people do, but I
do because of the exile, and we sit down
on the bed by the window and open the curtain
better to see the skyline, the river,
and whatever else we might have forgotten.
And the talking is difficult, though easier
for a certain numbness, and at some point,
after a long pause, you remove a thin instrument
and your hair falls down your shoulders
and over your breasts and I run around
turning out all artificial lights and I
expect that you might start to sing
but your expression changes in no way.

That night in the watery darkness
the moon fills your eyes
and as I float towards them time after time
I feel the miracle begin to happen all around;
the air moving like a liquid hand upon us,
then my sinking and sinking,
every atom slipping down,
down into a dark sea where, like phosphorescent fish,
tiny seraphim on little clouds made of the stuff
inside of pillows pass before me shooting-gallery style
blowing trumpets clear as Jericho or Judgment Day.

It's difficult for me to see that I'll require
either being stoned or broken
while around me falling stars share in my fate,
a comet flies like a flaming sword, and the moon
hangs very far away swinging like a slow pendulum.

A party of angels gathers to claim me as their own
and I am surprised at their crescent smiles
when I mention your name. So much revolves around us
I can hardly see you and I wonder whether you
are the fulfillment of a promise I misunderstood.

FOIL

"Never choose words for their sound." That day
the rhymed play, pauses and rhythms betray
your showy shallow slavishness, how beauty
draws you away from what you really had to say
and appears as what a listener was hoping for,
like the faceted glint of aluminum foil
to the raven's eye, the round plump
female feature to the guy, the darting lure
to the piscine predator, sparks of human
supplication sung to a possible deity
(what I fear my love for you might be).

IN THE OL' SWIMMIN' HOLE ONCE AGAIN

while I am bathing in my dreams
like mums or nuns in sunshine
a taxi pulls up outside
clouds skim the low sky
like stones water everyone's
hands are like shields are like shelter
aluminum awnings the rain off of
rings like a duck's back
the waterspouts rise on their tails
from the clinks of our tall icy glasses
the stereo wails this song
In the Ol' Swimmin' Hole Once Again
as my smile begins to precipitate
guests through doors and windows stagger out
to thine own self be true in my ears
in my arms you are floating at last
as those lonely people fall and hit the ground
to us like snowflakes touch a frozen lake
we want to be like when the weather's like this
only stay a while the music is so lyrical
with yearning please to lie alone
is winter ignorant of spring

YOU DON'T WANT TO WHEN WE MEET AGAIN

In silent, empty shoes the nights come running up.
We used to walk along the river counting in the current
and the dark sky innumerable lights by which to see each other.
These quiver and stick now in the pin-cushions you are
drawing from the back of a musty cupboard we discover.
We feel through our feet the scurrying of what we have
disturbed and we are disgusted by the quick, sharp teeth
we know are crawling in the walls. Our many matches
are streaming along cracks in the window panes as we find
the old radio cabinet with the sun and the moon, their faces
painted on, a smile and a frown. As my hand comes near
its smooth mahogany we hear the static of all the programs
sitting inside. A glistening spider web flickers near
the on-off knob. When I brush that away boards groan in rooms
we cannot see. Our matches are running out. When at last
I turn the radio on, the door crashes against the wall,
the wind rushes in like crooked old peasants with raised sticks
and beats out the light.

FOOD OF LOVE, PLAY ON

It is the anniversary of you as a secretary
in the office where you seek greater appreciation.
It is the anniversary of our wedding cake
and my professional ambitions.
Think of the odds against any of those
and another celebration is always sneaking up
and, meanwhile, every dinner I finish
is potentially dangerous. You laugh.
Salmonella. For six hours
after meats and perishable sauces
my stomach hides behind my crossed legs
waiting for twinges of pain to pass.
Everyone's amused at this,
my deadlines crawling through my guts:
"More likely you'll be struck by lightning"
and you, "More chance that elves
will write your great book in the night."
I have to smile, of course.
Botulism: to be dying 18 or 36
hours before one's vision splits,
before things are difficult to swallow,
before one understands
the stiffness in the neck is spreading.
But the electric sky just last night—
the thickest clouds broke, lit up
and I am wondering.
Ptomaine you have convinced me
is avoidable;
the food would be rancid to the tongue,
stinking, plainly pathogenic, intolerable.
When someone mentions that one
we hold hands and I feel safe,
as safe as I can be.

CALL

phone-, mail-, photo-,

close-, hard-, too close to-,

casting-, cattle-, curtain-,

bird-, battle-, booty-,

-to arms, -and raise, -for help,

distress-, last-, final-,

love-, wake up-, love-,

-waiting, -forwarding, -waiting

SIX COMPOUNDS OF AN ELEMENT

1. At the Entrance to Great Wildlife Preserves

At the entrance to great wildlife preserves
the quantum shifts are different when you
step from unbroken sunshine on to the crackling leaves
and walk into the Pennsylvania forests or the
foothills of the mountains of Montana and Wyoming,
and the herded plains of Africa spread out before
you like a map from luscious life on the hoof
to death inevitable in all its slow and sudden
forms and back. But at the entrance, entering the park,
your heart will register that measurable uptick
that tells you this is special, pay attention.
That is when the voice of Buddha in as many
decibels as necessary advises you that your
reaction is exactly what it must not be
and I don't know what you experience then
but what I see is the photo of Terri
on the date I first saw her that has sat in my brain
for some specific number of days and will for
all the days remaining in which she is wearing
a very prim suit, her shirt collars pinned with a brooch,
and an aura, for which there is undoubtedly an intensity metric,
of challenge and promise in the level stare
of those two, dark forbidding eyes.

2. Rx

When Terri is traveling and I open my eyes in the morning without her
I see the horizontal rectangle of the TV monitor and the vertical rectangle
of the bathroom entrance molding and threshold and next to that
the rectangles of the drawers in the file cabinet, the whole cabinet,
the basket resting on it and the frame, matting and image hanging above it,
and through the bathroom entrance, the tall rectangles of its partly open door,
its body-height mirror, the reflection in that of the towel hung on the shower frame,
and beyond those, the vertical portion I see of the tub I know is horizontal,
above which the blood-colored towel is draped on its bar like a flag below
yet another vertical black and white rectangle frame, matting and image.
All I see of the windows on the wall to my right are the rectangles
of their molding and 12 panes a piece, at least sixty rectangles
each in those apertures, then there's the bookcase between them,
the landscape of regular shelves and their uneven vertical bookends
all rectangles now and the walls and the ceiling and the floor
and the bed that holds me and shapes its own rectangle to me
as I lie stretched out beneath a blanket that insists on its rectangularity
since not conforming this morning to the hills and valleys of Terri's body.

How could I not be reminded of the fast days---of Upvas, Uposatha,
Yom Kippur, penitence, abstinence, Lent, of the Ramadan
or the transport of whirling past dizzy and chewing peyote to open that door
of the line in the software that sometimes reads "reset" and sometimes "refresh"
while that reptile rectangular hardware key just says "escape,"
and I can't help but think there'd be something to gain
were that start-over unit to read:
for the shock of awakening lonely,
for the stripping away of everything comforting,
for the deprivation or loss to you that holds the potential for addiction or freedom,
for that little whirlpool between reset and refresh that has to be swum somehow,
for mustering the weapons of the outgunned body
in its serial wars with the big geometrics,
for cleaning the lenses you wear as you walk
among the cruel beauties of the world.

3. Men of Mystery

In Terri's dream, the conference begins with a big cocktail party.
A young man with dark, curly hair steps assertively
up to the fancy hors d'oeuvres buffet
and announces My name is Jeffrey Tater.
She thinks about the origin of that. His grandfather
might have been some variant of Potato or Dictator;
those Ellis Island interviewers were notorious
sloths as well as jokers, she recalls, but here
they might have masked proclivity for porridge
or for power in the genes of Mister Tater,
who declares he has two children,
one three, the other ten.
The three-year old boy, he says, is a handful
but the other one he does not talk about,
does not even give a sex, making Terri wonder
whether something is evolving very awkwardly there,
along with a frisson of remembrance
that every adolescence takes place in a bad dream.
Then Terri and Tater are joined at a table
by the stylishly dressed and slender Daniel Schwartz
whose close-fitted suit makes him look quite successful
and at the same time on the make for a new job.

You can see from the table out into the garden
through which Terri had walked to the hotel front door.
The hotel turned out to be several small buildings
cobbled together with a warren of halls that went
different directions than one would expect;
you can see down one corridor maids cleaning rooms,
down another are waiters delivering food,
down a third barefoot swim-suited guests with their towels
and children wend their way to the pool.
T recalls climbing stairs, guessing which halls went where,
and descending again to the restaurant, which boasts
brick walls, dark wood floors, German beers, a rathskeller motif,
and there on each table attendees and guests
are tasting, then dining on, a huge wheel of brie.
She feels like a giant cheese herself, inexplicably.

Meanwhile, I lie quiet as a bunny,
twitching my little nose and wondering
whether I could touch her here and there
without waking her up and, as my rodential
qualities take over, whether, even if she
did stir momentarily, she might forget tomorrow
that it happened. Yes, forget tomorrow.
Play huggable rabbit, play adorable squirrel,
infiltrate the soft, somnolent landscape,
you sly rat in camouflage, and nibble away.

4. Stopping by Value Village on a Snowy Evening

We weren't sure why we decided to go inside at all,
but we had just rounded the corner from Aisle 3 –
painting frames, photograph albums and plates
calling out to us "Fill me! Fill me!" and were
heading into kitchen utensils, pots and pans, glassware,
"We can cook! We can serve!"
when God spoke to us
from a plastic Halloween pumpkin head
on the next-to-the-bottom shelf
between uneven stacks of wicker fruit baskets.
It seemed misplaced,
what with bird-bath Ganesha enthroned in a lotus,
shiny ceramic Lucky Cat raising a welcoming paw,
and wood carven falcon-faced Horus
all hobnobbing two aisles away,
but evidently was right where It wanted to be.
When God spoke, I thought the pumpkin head
glowed a little, but Terri said no, she thought
it moved side to side, when emphasizing,
but I didn't see that. Anyway, our ears
filled up with the very clear instructions
from the deep voice, almost like it came
from within us. "You are artists now.
Be artists. Ignore what they call you
and your creativity – primitive, naïve,
art brut." (I liked the sound of "art brut,"
and I could hear Terri's thoughts---she did, too.)
God, however, was focused and on a roll:
"When you are making your art, you are
doing My work in the world. So, get to it.
Ten four. Over and out. Leave the pumpkin head."
Terri immediately began collecting board games,
small animal figures ceramic and plastic, miniature
household items, doll houses, fish tank accessories.
"For boxes," I heard her think.
 "I'll call them 'Flora and Fauna.'

49

They'll be meditations on holistic living"
and off she went propelled to toys and games aisles,
while I was mesmerized by push-pins and clothes pins
and jig-saw puzzle pieces, Legos and pipe cleaners.
I was transfixed by bright visions of textures
created by multiple small things and shaped
into almost but not recognizable forms,
then displayed on the walls, floors and ceilings
of galleries suffused in primary colored light
cycling the rainbow every five minutes.
Shopping carts filling up, we had the same moment
a premonition that God was preparing to speak again;
back to the pumpkin head we rolled and there it was
shining as if in a spotlight and almost discernibly
shaking with energy, "Listen up, artists, do not forget
to be good citizens – vote, donate, volunteer, yadda
yad, yadda yad, yadda, you know what I'm saying,"
and we realized that we did and we had forgotten.
Terri and I both thought, "Thanks, Lord.
All we ever wanted was cosmic permission
to really be artists" and we laughed aloud,
people started to look and God, that Joker,
turned off the spotlight, said, like a throw-away line
even though in that big booming voice,
"Pumpkin head's getting old"
and took off for parts unknown.

5. The Tango

I had to agree with the close friend
who told me in anger and so
in the form of an unflattering insight
that I liked best what I did well:
billiards, poker, basketball,
washtub bass, politics, poetry;
perhaps because I understood these things,
but more likely because I could
dominate or be preferred.

And what could I say to the charges
of collecting and hoarding
and knowing the names of things
and visiting places and wanting to win
and to do things with skill—and be liked,
all of which I recognized as facets
of that most dense jewel: vanity,
but guilty?

Many dances are attractive to possess:
salsa for joy, waltz for permanence.
Late in life, I saw the tango.
Which I could not understand;
at which I would always be a novice,
impervious to any investment of time;
had heard the music, but had never
imagined the presence of bodies
completely committed to doing it
as if anything less than everything were nothing;
and could never hope to call my own.

As a teen and in her twenties,
my love exists to me only in photos:
young, lithe, effortlessly graceful
in line, jazz masterpiece of features,
an object of endless contemplation.

Then years and years of business suits
and severe, ambitious, perfect hair.

At fifty, she became fabulous, blond,
gliding in slacks and very shaped raiment.
For whom she did this, I have no idea:
for me, for someone else, herself;
suddenly a stranger in my skin,
I found I didn't care. And haven't since.
I don't know why I don't care;
as the one in my position,
I imagine that I should.
But I don't.
I wouldn't say that I've been stupefied.
I'd say that gratitude uplifts me like a tide.

Perhaps some grand pattern
will be revealed to me, like the melody
from an overture, the key from the tonal row
that winds among the flowers of dissonance
like slate steps through the English garden.
Or perhaps the winner is the self I'll never know,
the one who taps me on the shoulder
when I want to understand
some essential mystery such as love.
"Pardon me,"
the insincere, insistent voice intones,
and I must step aside
or be thought less of.

Naming the bright, searing union
of life and death "lightning"
or any word
always seemed the epitome of delusion
to me and ironic as any attempt
to herd the whirlwind:
calling the flaming sunset "beautiful,"
labeling the tree exploding with leaves,

saying over and over and over
the name of the lover;
I'm asking whether it's our salvation,
at last, that violence
is not the only failure of language.

There's something that I'm struggling to admit
and I just hope it doesn't mean
my close friend understood me well enough
to verify that I've become a worse than average fool:
Of all dance, tango is my favorite.

6. Ne Plus Ultra

My mother told me everyone does something
better than anyone else in the world.
I doubted that and doubted she believed those words
herself, but understood that she was telling me to find
that unicorn vocation for myself. I wondered, feared,
the talent of my excellence would be
to balance peas along a knife in number and longevity
beyond what anybody currently could conceive.
With a curious perversity I actually gave that a try,
but it turned out I wasn't all that good with peas and cutlery.

I'm motivated by the legendary charm of young Joseph Schumpeter
who stated his goals were to be the Greatest Lover in Vienna,
the Greatest Horseman in Europe, and the Greatest Economist
in the World, and later claimed two out of three while adding
off-handedly that he and horses never did agree.
For better or worse, I learned to settle for pleasure
rather than some more objective, competitive measure
and all that's sweet of teaching, working, public service
has been mine. There is possibly a policy, program
or presentation I have crafted that outshines all others,
but if I could choose how to make my mother's prophecy true,
I'd be dusting off for you with the world's falsest modesty
my Nobel Prize for being best at loving Terri.

DEFINITION

so we
like cool winds in rains
and rains on days
and days on days
and layers of days on time
like folds on fans
and pleats and prints on
gaily whirling skirts
(in all these ways)
begin
and must
before the swirling settling
of our dust
inform
before becoming
them
old rains, old days
the fabric of the past
the woven joy
we have created
death we have defined

THIS FOR THAT

I never intended to write poems that tell stories,
at least not the kind of story that has characters
and a plot and sequential events with surprises
and an ending that resolves tensions,
as if the whole endeavor were a metaphor for sex.
Now, a sexual relationship is a different thing
because the tension never gets resolved
and requires not one but lots of metaphors.
Here's what I mean. When your lover
loses a sister or a brother, how with any
sense of clarity do you describe the pain
you feel? To a lover, how do you use
the tools of lust and touch and gesture
to convey that which you must—beyond
the things you have to say. You see,
the sex becomes a metaphor and not the other way.
Your fingers are a sculptor's gouge and file and brush,
your tongue trails over flesh a liquid narrative;
the pleasure that you give with pressure of your body
to the other's is metonymy for your identity as lovers.
Sex is the choicest simile to express how need
to overcome a barrier makes achievement sweeter
than an easy win, how pain and arduous gain
and desperation, gambling, risks, dependencies
and unimagined generosity are often thin distinctions.
How energetically we seek to manage mind and body
separately, how strenuously we fight rather than admit
the bond we cannot quit and struggle to control
with someone who has taken us beneath the skin
to share a hurt, connect our sadnesses,
distill from defeat's vast vat the liquor of a win,
to grieve, exult, console,
confess.

MIRACLE IN THE MARRIOTT

I wonder how it got to the 14th floor.
Did it start its climb from subterranean depths
through ducts and shafts, along pipes and beams
and cables, living on organic specks among the dust
that settle in the dark from floating in the thick air
like nutrients sinking beneath the surface of the sea?

Was it scouting on a block, pane, slab, façade,
pre-fabricated metal sheet, rolled insulation pad
and lifted up, away and into a new pandemonium?
Hijacked on a shoe, a sleeve, within a head of hair;
at some point did it take the elevator?

At first it seems impossible but ask around
and you will find that everyone has found an ant
as if it had been sent to them a courier
with the message you are not alone not ever
so much crawling life will never be denied
yes you are an individual but everyone is
billions are and you have found your way
this little room appointed for you is a destination
also for your ant be thankful you have not been cut
and displayed in the lobby on a vase under glaze
because you were so pretty.

The dandelion grows in the sidewalk crack
the indolent masses of moss hang around
the trees in warm moist climates and their
debutante cousin orchids are adapting each species
to a narrow band of temperature until everywhere
from the Amazon rainforest to the Himalayas is occupied
not only by them but armies organized so thoroughly against you
digging and flying almost enough to shake your faith
termites with their lumber loving buzzsaw biomes and mosquitos
with their host of lethal fevers and in case you do survive them

wasps are winging with allergens to sting awake
your own tongue's dormant appetite to grow until
it starves its cave of breath completely.

Somewhere on a now-sundered continent
something slithered from the sea onto shore
took a shallow breath then a deeper one
liked the new neighborhood more
staged with plush plant life and all
and claimed the lands of the planet for bugs.

I see its progeny marking the territory
pretty much like my dog does
lifting their thousands of legs
and tip toeing through dark moist passages
as we all have done at birth and ever since
avoiding the larger calamitous feet of others
enjoying their treasure of trash and droppings
with some combination of reflex and luck
as floods and lava roll around
and volcanoes compete with meteors
to author climate change abrade
wipe away and repopulate the world.

I know how odds work
evolution a product of big numbers
a lot of cards shuffled and a lot
of errant ants don't make it back to the farm
survival at millions against one still odds-on
in the jungle of a billion perhapses
cartoonish mistakes and horrific miscarriages

and yet on my lips and my fingertips
this fabric of poetry
feels more than random and
must be like honey to ants
or those pheromones that make them dance
along a line that could be confused with purpose

and when I look at you
sitting on the bed we are sharing
high above the milling people
small below as you know what
and you point to the insect sauntering on the sill
as if there would never come a cleaning
then my dear Royal Flush
the word miracle still has a meaning.

SIMILE

It is this way:
in the morning
with your kisses
on my eyes and lips
like dew
then the brushing by me
in your style
of the warm tresses of the sun
and the flowing tresses of the river,
the moon's silver tresses
and those of the silken wind.
You are, like such a day,
the passing beauty of all lovers
and I transcendent like a leaf.

The Occasional Poem

Falling backwards
from his boat, the diver would see,
beneath the surface busy with leaves and eels,
how the rivers don't seem separate after all….

---Aleda Shirley, "The Rivers Where They Touch"

THE OCCASIONAL POEM

Cape Cod, July 5, 1998

From time to time you see your face
in the mirror very clearly, so close
you look down into the black vase
at the center of each eye
and everything else is closed out
except the scenes in your life carved sharpest,
those household shrines of memory that flutter alive
like an old home movie reel,
like the heartbeat you notice.

And in one of these are the four of you,
sitting at the table on the deck in the bright Cape Cod sun
reading Aleda Shirley's poems aloud,
crying at the beauty of pearls, silk, and drowned lovers,
and what you know about yourself and of each other:
the mother framed in the doorway in her red blazer,
holding her martini glass and waving,
so proud to see in you her gifts of grace and elegance;
the common laborer, your great-great-great grandfather,
who never returned to his father's birthplace
where you now vacation when you choose;
the great-uncle jailed for hosting a potlatch
who taught you how your tribe invented its myths
to get by in this chaos with dignity, as you do;
only you know how hard they worked;
only you know the wealth you each inherited.

Other people plant other seeds
of hope and passion in your life
with a smile, a touch,
a hand on your shoulder or around your waist;
the tendrils of other joys and angers
hold places close that balance and sustain you,
but this, this is the occasional poem,

just for you and those most dear,
a small property with high fences and a little space to garden,
where you find your love for each other flowering
like the complex blossom of a luminous white orchid
set in a smooth and a dark
and a seemingly bottomless vessel.

FLIGHT

What a beautiful eye had the restaurateur
who first gave the groupings
 of gumbo, she-crab, corn maque choux
dry, extra dry and brut,
pineapple, Georgia peach, blood orange,
three sherries, three beers, three ports,
all the same lofty name as birds on the wing,
whose purposeful pattern gives meaning,
direction and focus to sky in its vast
separation of earth and the starry abyss.

CORING THE APPLE

This is my most radical poem.
I just name the metaphor
and leave it at that.

Because otherwise
there's always too much more.
Like you're riding on the metro
and then someone sits down
next to you and opens up their book
and you look at what they're reading
and the illustration reminds you
of a fairy tale your father made up
to fascinate you just enough to make you sleepy

but it seems that you have been distracted
from your own thoughts then your memory
does the opposite of make you sleepy
like a nighttime cup of coffee it's as if
you have entered a world of mistake.

I thought World of Mistake wow.
Re-title the poem this.
But that's not where I was going
so I didn't.

It's very fashionable now to justify
art by showing how many jobs it creates.
If this gets anthologized I expect that
there will be a lot more work to do
figuring out what the poem and the fact
it got selected say about America now
and the current state of literature.
I am sure at least one household somewhere
would be counted as supported by such work.

I am sure a metric could be visioned
for all the jobs created by a poem
and how readings publication criticism
increase employment exponentially
but people understand that don't they?
People know that when you pluck things
like a fruit
they will have seeds
like a fruit
and they can grow
and sometimes often really
you can hardly count the profits.

So that's why I'm not stopping everything
and calling this Counting the Profits
which emphasizes some points
but not others
(like the ones about the fruit)
and besides if I gave in to my
more didactic tendencies
it would ruin the whole deal
that it's not all about me
which I have to admit,
OK, embrace.

Someone is going I just know
to summarize this with the first three lines
as if they were a whole poem.
See, you don't even remember.
They go:
This is my most radical poem.
I just name the metaphor
and leave it at that.
Yes, those three.
The whole poem.
I just know this.
I suppose I asked for that.

Anyway, now you know
why I'm just calling it
Coring the Apple
and letting it go.

REPETITION

> Pete and Repeat sat on a fence.
> Pete fell off. Who was left?
> Repeat!
> Pete and Repeat sat on a fence….

Why is repetition rare in those terrains
where we can instead create anew, again and again?
Miles to go before I sleep—
Ou sont les neiges d'antan?—
Why so seldom do we choose to repeat?
Why so seldom return to refrain?

There are those who say love must be rare,
that appreciation gathers like jewels of dew on what we cannot spare
and water, water, whether still or stormed and roiling is a bore
without a firmly drawn horizon and a quoth of nevermore.
We vote with tired eyes and irritable fingers turning pages.
Rather than reiterate, we choose to climb to higher stages.

Others sounding equally as sage will swear
that love is never isolated. It is everywhere
a lover looks. It answers always, always can be found
by open eyes. The sea, the skies, the ground
are full of echoes. We don't repeat because we seldom need to.
We seldom need to. That is why we do.

GREENE STREET MURAL

---After the large Roy Lichtenstein wall painting

The mute pyramid, cloud burst, supine funnel and vertical smear of blood
pose like dancers voguing in a strobe light.
The composition notebook, slice of Swiss cheese and open folding chair
share a secret: whether they are full of human potential
or have been used and discarded.
From behind the floating red electrical cord and the stately file cabinet
an envelope protrudes that might contain
a bulletin, an agenda, an accounting
but for now and it seems like forever
the wide-eyed and clueless face peering in through the window
and all of us who are reading the familiar images
of our daily lives abstracted and displayed like cartoon wallpaper
are looking for direction
and we are on our own

THE SNAPSHOT OF YOUR PARENTS SITTING

He's right. She's left.
She is intent upon pointing out his mistake.
Her pencil points to the newspaper spread open
on the table top, but its tip and most of the paper itself
are out of (below) the picture.
He looks at her as if he can't believe it.
She looks at the pencil as she talks.
Her fingers touch the words she points to
as she talks, but he is looking at her
as if he were the one making the point
and as if he can't believe it.
All the kitchen appliances are out of focus.
The washing machine in the background
shakes itself into a blur as they talk.
The broiler rides the washing machine,
seems to be warming and softening, becoming
pliable as clay. The broiling pan is not inside
of the broiler, but sits on top covered with
wrinkled aluminum foil so food won't stick.
As he looks at her eyes, all the light
in the room begins to collect in the foil
and appears as many small marshmallows
melting into each other. The sink,
next to the washer, is barely distinguishable,
mostly blocked by your father's torso,
but the dishes in the full rack are recently washed
and as your father looks at your mother
as if he can't believe it, they heat, dry,
and yield up their light to the foil,
marshmallows melting, overflowing the pan,
about to spill onto the blurred washer
which vibrates heavily in the background
between your parents' opposing shoulders.
Shadows cover more and more of your mother's face,
but there is a shiny, lighted place on her forehead,

perhaps the residue of the snapshot flash,
perhaps a thin film of perspiration,
at which your father continues to gaze
as if he can't quite see it.

THE COMITY OF ERRORS

We thought he was going to cry,
or go blue with his held breath.
He just sat there washing his hands
over and over, without water. Then,
"Why can't you see what Shakespeare
is telling you, all of you, all a few,
all of ewe, a la vue, all a view,
Allah---phew! I love you, I love you,
I love you." We were frightened.
He was talking to his hands.
" 'O that,' you say, and it's nothing,
too much ado, adieu, adieu a dieu,
but couldn't you also say: O – it's the world;
the globe; the wooden stage that also is a world;
the French word for water; the fluid
of grace, birth, baptism, redemption;
'O know, sweet love, I always write of you…,
O truant Muse…, O thou, my lovely…,
O, for my sake…, O benefit of ill…,
O me! what eyes hath love put in my head,
which have no correspondence with true sight.'
How could he instruct you more directly?"
When he stopped washing, he placed his palms
flat on the desk, close together,
where he could see them,
and he was intolerably sad,
and lay his forehead, quietly, between them.
What a comedy of errors, I thought then,
to look hard unto madness
for what was never there.

HOW I DID NOT WRITE ELEVEN BOOKS OF POETRY

I had sex about 400 times.
Or I hung around hoping to have sex
about 400 times.
Or maybe I just didn't lie there
with a pad and pen or a laptop computer
hoping for inspiration
because I was afraid of being abandoned
or told I would have to leave
about 400 times.
Now, I'm not so sure whether the number
of these incidents is closer to 400 or 1200
but I'm pretty sure that's why I did not write
at least eight books of poetry.

Then there was the year I did not write
a poem per week.
Or, actually, the two years I wrote a poem
every other week.
So the one about the hatching of the robin's egg
and the one about the snow falling
with anthropomorphic intent such as claiming,
preserving or smothering (you know, a little bit perverted)
and the one where the night approaches like an animal
possibly domestic but more probably dark and beautiful
and wild and threatening and thrilling
all did not get written.
So that would have been another book.

And then the haiku,
one for each card in the deck of 52.
The beautiful leaves and boughs and branches
had already had their painting done so well
with drops of rain and glistening
and little ponds and bridges lovingly displayed.

I tried to update all the nature with more modern
urban images---the taxicabs, the cell phones,
asphalt streets pocked and puddled, traffic lights,
delivery vehicles. I was moved seeing connection
across continents and weather systems with umbrellas,
but I kept returning to the faces, upturned,
glancing, eyes averted for the most part.
There might be a book or more of haiku there,
but not from me.

And I have loved my body so uxoriously
I cannot count the poems I did not write
just lost in fantasy of running, being
at the bat or in the ring, and then I reached
a point where I actually did exercise
with regularity and never have stopped that,
so have to look at one more pile of poems
unstacked---at least another book.

Now that's eleven easily accounted for.
I can not say the world is much the poorer,
that the law of balance between matter
and beauty has materially been affected;
in fact, the various identities of beauty
may have been protected in the largest
scale and schemes in some ways
by my laxities and choices seemingly
without a purpose. This year the last
surviving three-ring circus folded down
its final tent. It made me wonder
whether there's a right or wrong
to thinking of the cost in centuries
of other ways all that time in wonderment
could have been better spent.

OBJECTIVE MEASURES
OR
HOW YOU RECOGNIZE THAT YOU ARE NOW
A REPUTABLE POET

You arrive by plane. Your long ago moment of thinking
O how well lit and safe the Pittsburgh bus stop is
has submerged, floated down and now lies at the bottom
of the Marianas Trench of your memory.
The airports start having more than one restaurant.
Your destinations start having better restaurants than the airport.
Someone meets you at the airport.
At least one in three times, that person is wearing a tie.
When that person is wearing a tie, it is not necessarily because
he or she has come directly from serving fast food.
At the majority of destinations,
attendance is neither obligatory
nor driven primarily by case-making for parole.
People fill some of the seats in the first two rows.
At your readings, at least two people look as if
it is both medically and statistically possible
that they might have sex that night.
One of them is you.
At your last two readings, no one in the room,
yourself included, developed a hacking cough.
At almost every reading, someone asks you to read a poem---
by its title---from a previous book.
During your last two readings, that person has not been
your accomplice graduate assistant, a former flame, or a blood relative.
After your reading, at least one aspiring young acolyte
waits to ask your advice about a writing program
and at least one other waiting
does not wear corrective lenses, and at least
one of the final congregants is willing
to purchase whatever it is you are currently selling.

WHY THE LAZIEST POET CONTEST HAS BEEN DELAYED

I am running the first competition for the laziest poet.
I am frustrated to discover I have invented a double dilemma;
namely, I could be a contender, but I'm now a promoter;
or, I could recuse myself, if I had the energy to recruit,
and train, and explain all the definitions to, a partner who would do it.
Bear with me if I'm rambling; that's what lazy poets do.
And lazy readers love to hear dilemmas other people have.
Don't you?
Who is lazier do you think—the poet who offers you three endings
or the poet who only gives you one? And is it lazier to rhyme or not?
Take your time. (Lazy readers, I know that you
are bending toward the option of a single ending.)
Meanwhile, I could claim the trophy, award it,
or deputize your vote on whom to bestow it,
the criteria being only two: one, *lazy*; the other, *poet*.

LIT COURSES ARE THE CRUELEST

I rue the day I saw the snake
and thought "What a narrow fellow!"
because, later, in class,
there's that line, hel—lo—o ,
I don't even have to say it,
do I? In the grass, in the grass,
in the grass! I know! And I
have spent many a Friday
as a recluse, you could say
that I am one acquainted
with the weekend blight,
the kind that's measured out
in coffee grinds, the kind
that crawls along the floor like
some bewildered arthropod of yore.
If I had just been born before the
Belle of Amherst, you'd be wondering
whether ever I had sex, with others.
In the spring I saw a flower blossoming
and I thought "that stem is like
a green fuse" ---that would have been
me! "Born too late" occurred
to me just now; there's no one
more original in phrasing things.
I'm thinking "once I could have been
the future king" and then I learn
another even said some thing like that,
but as I walked along the beach today
a thought flowed through me
like a turning tide: my job must be
to reinvigorate the ancient phrases—
and to make them new—
and that would be a consolation
doubtful to be witched.

Immediately, I heard words ring
above the waves and then I knew
that I would be the first since
bold Odysseus shook his shackled hair
to say, "Beware! Beware of me!"
(That's great, right? The same word twice!)
"For I have heard the mermaids sing
and drunk their melon cider spiced!"

PRAYER

I put it away for years
in a dark place
I hid it out of fear
I could not face
its finality
I did not have the will
to cut away each ultimately every
non-essential thing until
the emptiness had filled me
and my desperation led
where none had been admitted
where no glow could be
but imagined only hoped for
Yes I threw out all the images
touched seen tasted poor
is what they'd made me cages
dead leaves ashes had to go
with petals guide dogs cries of birth
You perhaps have come to know
that hunger of suspecting nothing worth
illuminating has been hidden
That specific doubt is like an appetite
without a mouth an auction bid in
blindfold flare out we are scouts
the deathly night around us
rubbing words with words to kindle light

DEAR DYING POETS

Why do you craft your most beautiful rafts
after you know the currents are all pulling
out and away to the distant, barren beach?
Why do you hold on until we know you
better than ever and have a sense already
what it is we'll miss about you most?
If only you could settle on a price,
we'd pay, and then you'd get one more
extension, one more leave left open-ended.
We cannot ever be consoled once time,
that thief, has put your final sweet into
his list, once no more your beauty sails
the ships home from the foreign shore,
once your hand no longer bends
our step to steady, and all the rivers
of all the days run into sand or eddies.
Most frustrating to me is that I cannot grieve
full throated without end as you decline
and start to be more ready to depart
because I am so angry with the false choice that
you leave between imagined worlds of meaning
and a truth requiring make-believe.

HOMAGE TO W.S. MERWIN

This poet cultivated a paradise of palm trees
with seeds collected from around the world,
settled down in a town on Maui
with the hyphenated name Haiku-Pauwela,
all the more magical since haiku
in Hawaiian doesn't even mean a poem
and there in the place name is that of his wife,
Paula. Also, the name of the Merwin Conservancy
director is Sonnet (yes, Sonnet!) Coggins
and this winner of a couple of Pulitzers wrote
"This must be what I wanted to be doing,
Walking at night between the two deserts,
Singing." And after his principled,
sharp-worded war protests,
his cumulative portrait of a here-and-gone cosmos
impassively open to being defined,
a *Washington Post* writer gave voice in a flattery
to our collective jealousy, observing
"he was helped along, perhaps, by his handsome,
square-jawed, appearance." What can we say?
Some people have all the luck and still do a good job.

(1927--2019)

THE ARRANGEMENT

> She, who led me where she would is gone,
> So when he calls me, Death shall find me ready.
> from "To My Ninth Decade," W.S. Landor

the wonder is for whom
we write our poems
beyond the ears
of lives and the beloved
dust may come from stars
and may be stars again
but dust is what outlasts
we have the clippings
of the news in which
the poet W.S. Merwin
is "famously handsome,"
and another describes his
"extravagant handsomeness"
"tomorrow" he said
belongs "to no one" and
whenever he arrives there
"everything is changed"
the way I see it
dust re-arranges dust
for dust
in service to the dust
in that is poetry
without which
the dust is everything
so be it

CLEARING

if I had it to do all over again
I would gather to myself fewer
of everything and attend more to each
for no matter how much love
you think you have to offer
it never is enough to reach
as wide or deep as you can see

surprise in wide: too soon expended
surprise in deep: extended endlessly
it is not easy to love everything
or to perceive a world reciprocating

wisdom I find difficult to parse
regret is such a participle
of experience it is the verb
that acts as adjective in retrospect
the joy of knowing how it might
have better been is sharp if brief
being so long in the making

short knife whittled down
from fresh cut wood
one blade slicing out another
that's an image for it

the bag of skin we travel in
grows tough   it is because of all
the friction   there are no sad poems
only those reminding us of why
we want to stay and those
that melt away even as we say them

thirsting slaking blooming bursting
walking building fences difficult to tell
contrariness resolved from seriatim
keeping out from keeping safe

the point is what is keeping all about
participle adjective from gerund noun
exploding from perpetuating   what it was
from what it is and will become and always
ambiguity one cannot be too clever
here's the little forest clearing
kitchen courtroom where we seed
slice litigate for growing cooking
winning more than nothing should it be
that both our living and our dying are forever

THE POEMS WE DO NOT WRITE

Somehow, they get written.
Sometimes through metaphor
the anger burns its chemical way
through wood or metal instead of flesh,
the sorrow bends a rain-soaked branch or
slowly lowers the head of an animal in the background.
Sometimes the indigestible just forces its peristaltic
way into words like the anguished conversation
you have with yourself about the time your mother
took your hand, wanted you to feel her hernia,
but you couldn't do that for whatever ineffable
reason that you regretted instantly
and forever after, having divined
she wanted to be touched and maybe
only in that way by only you.
Sometimes the poems about your bowels,
your bladder, your other embarrassing urges,
the privileged intimacies with loved ones
never make it to the paper
or the screen; they turn into
incantations, prayers, just
a single step above, beyond or under
hopes and fears, one more articulation
of the bloody body's burden,
even in the fraction of a smile
angled with irony, confession,
derision, sympathy, the passions
you can name and those you can't;
somehow, they do get written.

THE FORMULA

Pick a word that denotes an admirable quality
of human interaction. Kind, considerate,
generous, exciting, the many kinds of calming,
soothing and consoling and their like will do.
You could try wondering, loving, empowering.
Think something wonders at something,
Something does something to something lovingly.
Apply it where we don't expect, like
between inanimate objects. Do it twice.
Then ask a question: where do you and I
apply it? Now make a statement about how
it must apply in the big, big picture of things.
And say why it does, has to;
what happens, what's left, if it doesn't.
Then go small, tighten the focus to an image
of this quality happening where it would
not have made sense before you showed
how it must.
Why does this formula work so well?
Is it because poems are vessels of yearning
and what you fill them with picks up that flavor?
Is the universe so empty that any pattern
of observation stitches it together with meaning?
Is the universe so full that when you unzip it,
coins from purse, the meaning spills out opulently?
Or perhaps all the suppositions are only superstitions:
the so-called laws apply here on occasion, there not;
causes abound, effects sometimes have them,
so which ones are only phenomena, who knows?
Your poem, that shooting star, incinerating
in the flash of friction with thin air,
is the brightest object of its moment,
refusing to fall to earth.

Bubbles

Find your mortal world enough

---W. H. Auden, "Lullaby"

HOLY GHOST

Somewhere in the recent past the Holy Ghost became the Holy Spirit.
I completely understand; "ghost" denotes what is not there.
"Spirit" says what is, as in inspire, the breath,
the breath that giveth life, life everlasting.
I know a bogus etymologist when I inhabit one.
I love words, but the words I write are what they mean to me.
And I'm not good at changing with the change of etymology.
For instance, I am still in love with ghosts.
So many of the ones that I hold close have moved along in spirit
literally; they live no more, but I continue to adore,
to love them as they used to be,
to love them as they were to me.
There are no better words for each of these I still hold close,
closer than most who eat and laugh and breathe,
for those who don't exist but never leave, than Holy Ghost.

SPORT

A man is hit at the line and a step behind from the start.
The end of the play is a slow, flying stretch for a ball
that rests on his fingertips where he will see it forever
and topples end over end as his feet go out from under him
and he feels the other's arms tighten around his waist.
Whenever we make love, we pay homage to his dumb pain
and its unfairness as we cry out,
as we scrimmage in our separate happiness together.

THE EGRET

stands among the rushes in the pond
perfectly balanced and does not respond
to breezes or clouds or anything that we can see
until it scoops a minnow up
like lightning cleaves a tree
and with a quick head shake
begins digesting it before it's even dead
and then the bright sunlight
seems to shift perceptibly
along its spectrum towards the red.

FALL

away like the light, dry leaf
sledding down its cool path of air
that time of year in temperate climes
when sap is slowing in the veins
of trees and xylem stiffens,
old men stumble, lose their
balance, of the annual metaphor,
spring is that part so far off
the cycle tips on the way down,
grace is what you reach for
as the sense of the divine
withdrawing all the underpinnings
deepens, your Eastern eye grows wide
in order to accommodate enlightenment,
never has your love of the world's
material things been stronger or more
precarious, little bird I see you
in a corner of my vision flutter like
you know what you are doing, dive
long and lovely as a maiden's tress,
your trail fills behind you like a watery torrent,
it occurs to me that many poems
have sung that swoop, neither sad
nor joyful, here and now I wish to know
all that there is to know of welcome and goodbye.

TOMORROW

a cloud covers the moon with its wing
the stark and monumental rabbit
disappears in the grey field
a freight train tracks the river
towards the city of your birth
worlds the color of bullets
fly into the sleeping imagination
of wild animals who with your children
envision a dark rim and golden dawn
while the fear that waking life
is just as much a mystery as dreaming
has you circling like a hawk
beneath a rushing sky

PATHETIC FALLACY

Towards a kiss for the spring returning like a lover in a wintery year,
your tribe of seasons push you forward from behind.
This parting of your lips will not be sunny
but like the musty awakening of fern spores
long dormant in the log's dark marrow
beyond the crystal fingers of the cautious forest moon.
The thawing world presses you closer, winds and rains
begetting misty evenings mingling
to bear the prodigal dew that seeks
its rest on softening river beds, trees, leaves
and, pendant under petals, makes their glad tears of relief
for the frozen clutch of the ground relaxing,
the distant breeze that news of the next frost rides.

PIGEONS

his birds circle the tenement roofs
she sits by the window in her living room
and her eyes turn down from the sky
he raises his arms and his birds come home
they are the objects of his special concern

she does not expect online thieves in the Ukraine
to target such small wealth as she has stored up
but who knows after all she buys lottery tickets
at neighborhood liquor stores takes yoga and signs up
to guide tourists because that's how you meet people

another man's hands are soft and smooth
but he buys a suit the color of cinder blocks
because he's in love it is late in the day
some are luckier than others and this man
enters a revolving door as he leaves work for home
and when he is outside alone on his street
he sees the birds above break their big loop
and angle down and the image lingers
like a lasso that did not reach a cloud

THE LIMITS

There are severe limits
to what you can do
about that body of yours
and you can spend a lot
of breath on those indignities
but the death that is life
without meaning, you have to
ask, is that possible,
and what can you do
about that

FORTUNES

> Kids can easily write a list poem
> using the process of observation.
> ---https://imaginationsoup.net

You will be presumed innocent.

You can be as good as your teachers expect.

If you work hard, you can pay the bills.

Your streets will be safe if you keep to yourself.

No one will focus on your petty crimes.

There will be enough air for everyone.

Something bends towards justice.

You are the future.

A list can easily become a poem.

ELEGY

for Dan Harpole, 1955--2006

I wanted words to say enough,
to buy the perfect gift,
to give sufficient funds,
a song of blessing from my lips,
the gesture most appropriate,
to bend a knee or bow my head,
to pitch my voice with an emotion
so precise and unmistakable, that
it would encompass what we have shared
and are afraid of losing.
And now you know how short I've fallen.
There is one thing I learned and have to offer
as the fruit of this frustration:
the ground, the air, the sun,
the rain, are resonant with metaphors,
so many are the sights and sounds
of our contending celebration and our pain,
but they do not and can not contain
what must be sought to say,
and what surprised me was that this
is not about some blossom falling
from a tree of mystery. It's a
commonplace and household phenomenon.
It's the dialogue within you;
that's where it all continues
and does not end with light of day.

CARMELEE

Late in spring the air seems quite as clear
as it can be, the sky and birds and clouds
so close and easily understood that almost all of us
take stock in what we have and how it's good.
When one you love says you and this and all the world
are not enough, what can you do? Have you a choice?
She is as close as any sky and cloud
and clear to you as your spring was to her.
The spring will turn to fall and winter no consent from you
and all you may remember are a spreading tree, a wandering star,
someone you wanted happier. If everything is not to fade,
what can you do but go on loving what had brought you joy?

OPEN SPACE

After the text at the end of my book were the empty
rectos and versos and they totaled two times four
so I wondered if maybe a law governs pages
because of the way paper folds or is bound
so no matter the stock, whether new or recycled,
the number is quartet and no less nor more.
I explored again my library differently than before.
It is a rare person who sews pages together,
who becomes the creator of his or her own book
in that way, page by page, stitch by stitch.
How fortunate it would be for your story to conclude
right at the bottom of the appropriate page.
I know, for most of us, that when the tale we are telling ends
some mute blank sides remain.
It would be presumptuous to mark this final territory
with a pre-planned valedictory, so it would be
a space for comment or summation or intention
or shoulda-coulda-woulda might-have-been,
but against the use of open space for notes by others,
there is neither argument nor defense, nor saving face
and laws have their own reasons, their own saving grace,
though I could not find proof of one, finally, in this case.

SILENT PARTNER

They say without her close at hand that
beauty is too bright a light forever shining in your eyes
and grace a phone that rings throughout the night,
that youth evaporates more quickly, time becomes
a hateful residue of spots and folds and noises,
sycophant lust and flattering strength,
your Rosenkrantz and Guildenstern—
without her, none to write the note
that lays them low at last.

You can't shake her sense of humor
when she dresses like an old guy
and swings that hefty scythe
around and every which way
or her veiled allure
aloof on the throne
of another world—
one that's free of tears and judgment.

Silent partner, what an image,
bell withholding clapper,
stopper tongue in bottle throat,
sneaking up on little cat's feet,
melting like a witch in water all around,
her gentle, iron grip upon our elbow
now a rudder steering us to hallowed ground.
If ever such a colleague uttered words
what would we have them say
in cloudy signal smoke or burning raspy crackle,
whisper, bang or thunder?
The dreadful thing about a silent partner
who might really start to talk:
what they would say and when shut up
could empty or could fill a universe of wonder.

WELCOME, STRANGER

In the end, some wounds don't heal.
Their damage continues.
There is no place they do not hurt.

Kathy will always be missing.
Every image and sensation will always
be less vivid without Leidy to see it
or Frank's enormous laughter at it
or Gary's wry, ironic reframing of it.

We are reminded of that special wound---
youth flying away---that never heals,
that serves the purpose of reminding you
that what you thought would be the worst
will actually be (you and those you love
will finally agree) relief.

In the family of experience, memory
is your younger, weaker sibling
who benefits on occasion from a pill
or potion.

Because wounds can be categorized
does not mean there is a category
where they are not doing what they do.

Memory is like a wrapping paper
printed all over with It was Worth It
It was Worth It It was Worth the Loss
Inside the box of gifts are
Kathy's determined good will,
Leidy's wide smile and cautious optimism,
Frank's infectious confidence and Gary's
push to get at least the obvious stuff done.

This is not to minimize the power of poetry
to imagine and contain and give a shape
to wounds, their causes and the nature
of their healing. It helps to see and say
something when you want to. Helps
to be precise and choose your audience.

And so you can't resist a crooked smile of arrival
when you saunter through the swinging doors
and that eternal bartend slams the shot glass down,
says, Welcome, Stranger. Name yer poison.

THE STARS SHINE

they are not mine
as metaphors
they're more like Yours
in that their glow
so steady and so slow
takes on the tour
of what they lit millennia before
as sounds they would be laughter
at the trivia of suffering sapiens after
so much time and distance
and their multitudinous dance
their stately waltz across the onyx
floor of heaven to which nothing sticks
you radiant dimples in the myriad cheeks
of dark and faceless smiles Who speaks
through your amused indifferent gaze
is there no Personality that plays
above the silence of rotation in the waves
breaking on rocks and shores and in the caves
that echo every condensation drip
and creature's splash also from every lip
and tongue and throat the utterances
of praise or hope or hunger What says
It listens says dross and baubles of the spinning years
be damned says everything created It hears

ENVIRONMENTAL MOVEMENT

my friend Merrill wrote a *cento* out of quotes
from fifty different writers it occurred to me
that were I to aspire to read an opus
by each one I would undoubtedly expire
before completing that task and my scientist
friends would be required to explain my
death was only *correlated* with my lofty
literary goal and not *caused* by trudging
up that mountain of uneven pleasures
which might or might not be true
since arbitrary goals can actually kill you
at first I thought that *cento* might have meant
a hundred and I would have been forgiven
not to try because too obviously daunting
but no---*cento* is from Latin meaning patchwork
sometimes you read each and every page
and yet your favorite magazine
fails to produce a single poem or essay
that speaks to you and then again
your bent and beaten pan turns up
a glint a nugget by the time you've
worked on it a semiprecious stone
you have to calculate return investment
labor and materials in all things alas the lack
of information at the moment is the
ointment's fly the world's supply
of metaphors is endless where each applies
how they connect who knows
you're in a cave spelunking can't go back
that commonality this passage has with time
reach for the hand beside you
breathe deep take another step

TRAVELOGUE

The child looks up.
He opens his hands above him
like Japanese fans, and crosses them,
but the sun pours in between his fingers.
It is too much. He blinks and runs.

Leaves rustle many years later and he hears them,
slaves dipping their oars and wishing to pull loose,
to overcome their links, to conquer rolling oceans
as the captains of their galleys.

It is an old man who recognizes the ancient blue mosaic:
through the glazed web of branches, sky after sun-shower.

Once, he looked up to find himself stretched out
upon an open, grassy field. Beside him,
where an elm tree might have been, a woman sat,
her patient fingers tracing simple patterns on his chest.
She smiled and said: A fare for every voyage.
He saw her as if through tears,
the sudden rain shining in her hair like honey,
its last golden coins lying wet and warm upon his closed eyes.

DEGREES

setting off and up so many as to indicate the steep incline
of your research to earn that academic highest
your eyes open your thoughts pushing out
your body abandoned sits in the British Museum
in hand Blake's copy of Swedenborg's *Divine Love and Wisdom*
with penned corrections in the margins
so now you know how deeply Blake's imagination
burned through flesh to pare back and reveal
his three layers of perception natural intellectual and spiritual
this last which he would stoke fire up and redefine
as genius yes poetic yes prophetic distinct from the other two
this third to apprehend God as a furnace and bellows within us
the royalty tinder and tinder the church of obedient worship
tinder the rule-bound flesh of the body
tinder the numbered and measured and marketed world

one unit Centigrade of ocean makes El Nino wet death here
and desert dry death over there while everywhere
the heavens open over narrow paths for life on earth
a few small steps each way in any one of several dimensions
swallows up the rooted and the grasping and the empathetic species
petrifies and prints the fossil record of the ones who otherwise
might have graduated found new work proved worthy of preserving
an interval of pH and the billion-bodied reef of coral crumbles
can you name the number of the less than perfect heart beat

I think at times like this how little of your mouth
would have to move for me to yearn the pattern of a smile
whether something from your eyes would be enough to recognize
what fraction of a decibel of irritation in your voice unbalances me
what scale of comparability do I not insult
what level of incompetence in art fail to reveal
what human weakness do I not betray
calibrating tragedy and starlight through a lens of mundane love

BUBBLES

Walking along in the crowd of the downtown the capital city
the national capital so many people flow with you
flow past you across you at corners come up from the Metro
descend as a snapshot we all are like bubble wrap over
the sidewalk and streets but each bubble is bobbing
I suddenly see me a bobbing balloon among many balloons
that are bobbing on shoulders and necks
each a consciousness globed in its own oblate spheroid
of luminous soap film, these ambient bubbles are bobbing
long rainbow-hued streams they are sliding in many
directions the patterns they trace weave a fabric
in motion kaleidoscope bubbles of consciousness
each with a life of its own percolating with ambitions
vibrating with recollections distractions the play of
the goals of associations after all it is Washington
bobbing the bubbles are currents agendas of policies
coursing and buoying these fragile containers of water and air
an emulsion miraculous how it evolved
from particulate elements hard to imagine
but this is the foam of humanity
was what I thought at that moment.
I was high above in my own streaming bubble afloat
looking down from my bubble of consciousness
at me and at all of the rest so ubiquitous
no more and no less than any of them evanescent
just high with advantaged perspective without knowing why
was it simply my time or my turn
I had never before seen more clearly.

Then I was grounded again in my cumbersome, robotic
body, its juggernaut bones, muscles, nerves and blood
plodding along. Gratitude, thought my bubble of consciousness
sitting aloft in its howdah of cranium, thanks, to the small elephants
at work in the center of atoms and the rogue elephants who mutate
genes with their clumsy feet into features that fit or decay.

What a treat to swirl air through a pair of lungs,
with another to jostle an atmosphere time to time,
to bounce word by word among fellow balloonists
afloat in their sentient moments of flight,
to take at least one breath as deep and as light as forever.
Thank you O pachyderm god O remover of obstacles
lord of reflection, of poems,
of numberless endless beginnings,
for lifting whatever I am through this physical world
that a vision of bubbles has burst my fear of leaving.

AUTHOR'S NOTES

p. 33, Food of Love, Play on

In *Twelfth Night*, Shakespeare's Duke Orsino, overcome by his passion for Countess Olivia, asks for an excess of music, the food of love, in the hope that "surfeiting,/The appetite may sicken, and so die." Instead of such a homeopathic approach, I had my speaker choose a full-blown phobia, and so my challenge became dramatizing how that, too, but differently, operates as a strategy for creating an emotionally safe haven.

p. 36, Rx

Each 12-pane window can be seen to have at least the following rectangles: 12 of 1 pane each, 17 of 2 panes, 10 of 3 panes, 9 of 4 panes, 7 of 6 panes, 2 of 8 panes, 2 of 9 panes, and 1 of 12 panes, not counting the rectangles with and without the center-panes as different from each other. The problem I set myself was to illustrate the way separation anxiety can manifest as obsessive quantification and abstraction.

p. 50, The Occasional Poem

The poem referred to is Aleda Shirley's "Speculations on the Pearl" in her wonderful collection, *Chinese Architecture* (University of Georgia Press, 1986). The two couples included our friends to whom the present volume is dedicated.

p. 55, Greene Street Mural

This is an "ekphrastic" poem, meaning an attempt to describe a visual phenomenon in words. Since artistry and literacy employ different symbol systems, this exercise can reveal as much about how perception and communication operate as it does about the artifact being described.

p. 56, The Snapshot of Your Parents Sitting

Also ekphrastic. The mysteries and inscrutability of even the most mundane moments can be represented just as vividly in either visual or verbal terms.

p. 76, Fall

This is one of what I call "dictionary poems." The challenge is to identify a word that has several seemingly unrelated meanings, then to create a coherence for those meanings in a poem without using that word, except as the title. So with "fall" one can work with the autumn season, a trip and tumble, a loss of power or position, water cascading, a hair extension, etc. See also "Flight," "Call," "Pigeons" and "Degrees."

p. 78, Pathetic Fallacy

While "pathetic" has ambiguous meanings related to feelings and to pitiful things, the "pathetic fallacy" is a jargon literary term for attributing human thoughts or emotions to an animal, plant or other non-human entity.

p. 79, Pigeons

A dictionary poem. See the note to "Fall." Dictionaries record that a "pigeon" can be a person easily fooled or the mark in a con game, a young or pretty girl, a blue gray color, and a card that helps a poker player or makes a winner.

p. 81, Fortunes

The more fraught with tragedy the news environment is, the more likely it is that a list, even a child's, will have the impact of a poem.

p. 82, Elegy

Dan Harpole dedicated his professional life to public service and to integrating artistic experience in community life. He chaired the Washington State Arts Commission, directed the Idaho Commission on the Arts, and was one of the elected presidents of the National Assembly of State Arts Agencies (NASAA) whom I partnered with as CEO. I recited this poem to those who filled the Egyptian Theatre in Boise to celebrate Dan's life.

p. 83, Carmelee

Carmelee Whitehead was my assistant director at the Kansas Arts Commission. Sharp as a tack, creatively funny, attractive, excellent at her work, admired and valued by friends and colleagues, she wasn't built to endure emotional setbacks.

p. 90, Degrees

A dictionary poem. See the note to "Fall."

p. 107, Environmental Movement

Readers can experience a *cento* by Merrill Leffler at takomaparkmd.
gov/news/together-we-by-poet-laureate-merrill-leffler
(2/9/2017 starting at 4:22).

ACKNOWLEDGMENTS

An earlier version of "The Lawn" appeared in *The North American Review*.
"The Object of My Affection" appeared previously in *REUNION: The Dallas Review*.
"You Don't Want to When We Meet Again" appeared previously in *Cottonwood Review*.
"Food of Love, Play On" appeared previously in *Kansas Quarterly*.
An earlier version of "Definition" appeared in *Quoin*.
An earlier version of "Degrees" appeared in *Nevada Arts News*.
"Bubbles" appeared previously in *Crazyhorse*.

Special thanks to Elizabeth Scanlon, Editor of *American Poetry Review*, for her generous and helpful advice in the preparation of this collection.

Cover artist Tarmo Watia can be contacted at tarmowatiagallery@gmail.com

C&R PRESS TITLES

NONFICTION
By the Bridge or By the River? Stories of Immigration
from the Southern Border by Amy C. Roma
Women in the Literary Landscape by Doris Weatherford, et al
Credo: An Anthology of Manifestos & Sourcebook for Creative
Writing by Rita Banerjee and Diana Norma Szokolyai

FICTION
A Mother's Tale by Kahn Ha
Last Tower to Heaven by Jacob Paul
History of the Cat in Nine Chapters or Less by Anis Shivani
No Good, Very Bad Asian by Lelund Cheuk
Surrendering Appomattox by Jacob M. Appel
Made by Mary by Laura Catherine Brown
Ivy vs. Dogg by Brian Leung
While You Were Gone by Sybil Baker
Cloud Diary by Steve Mitchell
Spectrum by Martin Ott
That Man in Our Lives by Xu Xi

SHORT FICTION
Fathers of Cambodian Time-Travel Science by Bradley Bazzle
Two Californias by Robert Glick
Notes From the Mother Tongue by An Tran
The Protester Has Been Released by Janet Sarbanes

ESSAY AND CREATIVE NONFICTION
Selling the Farm by Debra Di Blasi
the internet is for real by Chris Campanioni
Immigration Essays by Sybil Baker
Death of Art by Chris Campanioni

POETRY

How to Kill Yourself Instead of Your Children by Quincy Scott Jones
Lottery of Intimacies by Jonathan Katz
What Feels Like Love by Tom C. Hunley
The Rented Altar by Lauren Berry
Between the Earth and Sky by Eleanor Kedney
What Need Have We for Such as We by Amanda Auerbach
A Family Is a House by Dustin Pearson
The Miracles by Amy Lemmon
Banjo's Inside Coyote by Kelli Allen
Objects in Motion by Jonathan Katz
My Stunt Double by Travis Denton
Lessons in Camoflauge by Martin Ott
Millennial Roost by Dustin Pearson
All My Heroes are Broke by Ariel Francisco
Holdfast by Christian Anton Gerard
Ex Domestica by E.G. Cunningham
Like Lesser Gods by Bruce McEver
Notes from the Negro Side of the Moon by Earl Braggs
Imagine Not Drowning by Kelli Allen
Notes to the Beloved by Michelle Bitting
Free Boat: Collected Lies and Love Poems by John Reed
Les Fauves by Barbara Crooker
Tall as You are Tall Between Them by Annie Christain
The Couple Who Fell to Earth by Michelle Bitting
Notes to the Beloved by Michelle Bitting